fantastic ideas for
early language development

FEATHERSTONE

FEATHERSTONE

Bloomsbury Publishing Plc

50 Bedford Square, London, WC1B 3DP, UK

BLOOMSBURY, FEATHERSTONE and the Feather logo are trademarks of Bloomsbury Publishing Plc

First published in Great Britain 2018 by Bloomsbury Publishing Plc

A catalogue record for this book is available from the British Library

ISBN: PB: 978-1-4729-5601-9; ePDF: 978-1-4729-5600-2

2 4 6 8 10 9 7 5 3 1

Printed and bound in India by Replika Press Pvt. Ltd.

MIX
Paper from
responsible sources
FSC® C016779

To find out more about our authors and books visit www.bloomsbury.com and sign up for our newsletters

Acknowledgements

I would like to thank the staff and children at Lantern's Nursery School and Children's Centre and the reception class at Stanmore Primary School, both in Winchester. I am also very grateful for the help and support of Catherine Wharton at the University of Winchester.

Contents

Introduction

The main aim of the book

Language is one of the most important skills children develop in the Early Years. It contributes to children's success in all areas of the curriculum, as well as being essential for positive personal, social and emotional development. Many children are still starting their formal education with underdeveloped communication skills. Recent research has found that seven per cent of children struggle with speech, language and communication when they start reception. This equates to two children in every class of 30. This percentage is significantly higher in areas of disadvantage (The Communications Trust, 2017)[1].

There are a range of underlying issues that can affect children's language skills. A child who has impaired **hearing** will have less exposure to language than children who can hear well. Understanding language also involves being able to interpret visual cues, such as facial expression and gestures, therefore a child with impaired **vision** will not be able to observe these additional cues. If a child has a short **attention span** they may struggle to concentrate on what is being said, which may impact on subsequent language development. The ability to **distinguish similar speech sounds** is a key language skill and underpins the teaching of phonics. A good **verbal memory** is vital, as the brain must remember all the words in a sentence to make sense of what has been said, but a child may have difficulties remembering the string of sounds that make up a sentence. A child with underdeveloped **vocabulary and grammatical knowledge** may not understand the meaning of words or sentence structure.

The practitioner plays a crucial role in supporting and assessing early language development. In this book you will find a range of ideas to help you support such development. These ideas adopt a holistic and interrelated approach to teaching and learning and so the activities in this book cover all areas of the curriculum. Opportunities for assessment in each area are highlighted.

Many of the activities can take place both indoors and outside and they are designed to be playful, active and to promote creativity. The first set of activities involve gaining and maintaining young children's **Attention and Listening** and therefore are designed to help them tune in or focus on language, as well as encouraging them to hear, distinguish and remember sounds. The next set of activities support children's **Understanding** by helping them to make sense of the language they hear. The final set of activities focus on **Speaking** by encouraging children to put their thoughts into words and these ideas provide motivational and engaging contexts to use both their verbal and nonverbal communication. Whilst each section is designed to specifically focus on a particular area of language development, it is important to remember that the development of skills in these areas are interconnected, for example progress in Attention and Listening can impact on both Understanding and Speaking.

1. The Communication Trust, 'Talking About a Generation: Current Policy, Evidence and Practice for Speech, Language and Communication', available at: http://www.thecommunicationtrust.org.uk/media/540327/tct_talkingaboutageneration_report_online.pdf

Using this book

The pages are all organised in the same way. Before you start an activity, it's important to read everything on the page. Sometimes you may decide to change the order in which you do the activities or just pick and choose a game from the middle – that is allowed!

What you need lists the resources required for the activity. These are likely to be readily available in most settings or can be bought/ made easily.

Top tips give a brief word of advice that could make all the difference to the successful outcome of the activity, so make sure you read them!

What to do tells you step-by-step what you need to do to complete the activity.

Taking it forward gives ideas for additional activities to challenge the children and broaden their experiences.

What's in it for the children? lists some of the benefits the children will gain through the activities and how it will contribute to their learning.

Additional suggestions

If possible, try to carry out the activities in a quiet area. This will ensure that children can hear well and be easily heard. It is also important to remember your own role as a model listener and speaker. Additionally, when selecting children for some of the activities, it can be very helpful to consider the composition of groups. For example, ensure you have chosen some children who are good role models and have also considered the needs of children who are quieter and less confident.

Ready, steady, go!

What you need:

- An interactive toy like a spinning top, balloon, ball or a pop-up toy

What to do:

1. Find a quiet space to play where you will not be interrupted by loud noises or visual distractions.

2. Show the child the toy. Tell them its name and what it does. You might want to give the child the opportunity to touch the toy too.

3. You can get their attention by showing them how the toy works – use encouraging language and gestures while you do this to build excitement.

4. Once they start to become excited about the toy, build the anticipation by saying, 'Ready… steady…' and pause before you say 'go'.

5. Finally, operate the toy.

What's in it for the children?

Before they can listen and learn from the language you use, children need to learn to focus and pay attention to you. This activity concentrates on sustaining their attention.

Taking it forward

- Repeat the game a few times. Pause before you say 'go' and look encouragingly at the child.

- The child might use eye-contact, a gesture, a vocal sound or even the word 'go' to tell you that they want it to go!

Bubbles

What to do:

1. First, attract the child's attention by calling their name.

2. After you say their name, maintain eye contact with them and blow the bubbles. This is a great way to get a child to focus on your face and pay attention to you.

3. Model vocabulary such as 'pop', 'blow', 'big bubble' in between blowing the bubbles.

What's in it for the children?

This activity encourages children to focus their attention on you and watch while you carry out an action. It also provides opportunities for the child to start letting you know what they want.

Taking it forward

- Once you have played this game a few times, pause before you blow the bubbles to encourage the child to anticipate that the bubbles are coming. You might say, 'Ready, steady, go!' or '1,2,3, blow'.

- The child might try to communicate with you using their eyes, body language or speech to tell you they want you to blow the bubbles again.

Taking turns

What to do:

1. Get the child's attention by showing them how to play with the toy. For example, you could do this by gently taking the pieces out of the puzzle and offering them one.

2. Then, allow them to take a turn playing with the toy. Use their name when suggesting this, e.g. 'Jack's turn'.

3. Then, point to yourself and say, 'X's turn' and take a turn. Make the game exciting by clapping or using an excited face.

4. Repeat this process, taking turns to play with the toy, until the child's attention wanes.

5. When you have completed the activity, say 'Finished'.

What's in it for the children?

Taking turns is a really important early language skill. Not only does it help to develop children's attention skills, it is also the foundation of conversation.

Taking it forward

- Repeat this process with different toys to further encourage the child to take turns.

- Encourage the child to carry out this activity with another child to promote sharing and turn taking.

Visual singing

What you need:

- Suitable props for a simple counting song such as 'Five Little Ducks' or 'Five Little Men in a Flying Saucer': a set of rubber ducks with card or material representing a pond or a flying saucer and astronaut figures made of card (see photos)

What's in it for the children?

This a motivational way of extending the amount of time that a child can pay attention to an activity, as it is visual and has an exciting action at the end of every verse.

Taking it forward

- Repeat the activity with longer songs, or songs with more complex vocabulary, such as 'The Wheels on the Bus' or 'Old MacDonald had a Farm'. This will increase the length of time that the children can focus and pay attention.

- Regularly update the props you use to include an exciting range of artefacts and pictures, e.g. a baby doll, soft animals, paintings, art and crafts materials.

What to do:

1. Identify a small group of children as good role models.

2. Introduce them to the song using simple language and simple gestures. A possible gesture would be using fingers to make a quacking action.

   Five little ducks went swimming one day
   Over the hill and far away.
   Mother duck said, 'Quack, quack, quack, quack'
   And only four little ducks came back!

   Or

   Five little men in a flying saucer
   Flew round the world one day
   They looked left and right
   But they didn't like the sight
   So one man flew away
   Wheeeeeeeee!!

3. Sing the first verse and take the first turn yourself, e.g. remove a duck from the pond/an astronaut from the flying saucer. You can add extra features to the game to make it fun, e.g. the duck can drop into the pond and you all say 'Splash!'.

4. Then sing the next verse with the children or choose a child to come and have a turn, and so on until all the props have been used.

Sound detectives

What you need:

- Toys or objects that can make a continuous sound: a tape recorder, an alarm clock or a musical toy

What to do:

1. Ensure that you resource the environment with toys that can make a continuous sound. They should be easy to use so that the children can explore and listen to them independently, as well as when they are supported by you. The aim is to familiarise the child with the sound the object makes.

2. When you are confident that the children can recognise the sound of the object and have used it in their play, hide it somewhere in the room (make sure that it is making a noise when you hide it).

3. Ask the children to listen very carefully – they should be able to find the object by listening out for and following the source of the sound.

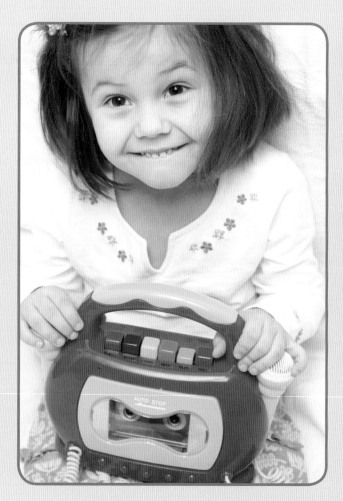

What's in it for the children?

This activity stimulates the child's ability to listen carefully. It also encourages them to distinguish where sound is coming from, which is a necessary skill that leads to being able to hear and identify specific sounds in words.

Taking it forward

- Give the children an opportunity to take it in turns to hide the toy for themselves.

- Link this activity to your topic by selecting toys with relevant sounds. For example, if focusing on 'Under the Sea' you might use the sounds of waves crashing or a whale song.

- Take this activity into the outdoor area. Encourage children to listen out for and follow outdoor sounds, e.g. birdsong, an ice cream van's chimes, car horns.

Joining the band

What you need:

- Age-appropriate musical instruments including a drum, shaker or tambourine

What to do:

1. Allow the children to play with the instruments as part of your continuous provision.

2. When interacting with the children as they explore and play with instruments, introduce associated vocabulary such as 'drumstick', 'beat', 'jingle', 'skin'.

3. Then choose two instruments and introduce an action linked to each instrument, like marching to the sound of the drum or running on the spot when hearing the tambourine.

4. Play a game where the children have to carry out the right action when they hear each instrument.

What's in it for the children?

This is a playful and active activity that can be carried out indoors and outside. It allows children to discriminate between sounds, as well as encouraging them to link sounds and actions.

Taking it forward

- Gradually introduce more instruments and associated actions, so children learn to listen for longer periods of time and can identify more sounds.

- You can also let the children be the leader of the band. Allow them to choose which instruments to play and to create their own associated actions.

Big ears!

What you need:

- Scissors
- Card or foam
- Headband or elastic
- Glue

What to do:

1. Make one pair of pretend ears for each child by cutting out ear shapes from card or foam and fastening them to a headband or piece of elastic with glue.

2. Take a small group of children outside the setting. Each child should be wearing a pair of 'ears'.

3. Ask the children to listen carefully and encourage them to identify the environmental sounds that they can hear.

4. Help the children by identifying sounds yourself and supplying the vocabulary, e.g. 'The leaves are rustling', 'We can hear the car's engine'.

What's in it for the children?

This activity can introduce children to lots of new vocabulary, in addition to supporting their ability to notice different sounds.

It is also a great assessment activity – you might become aware of children who seem to find it difficult to hear and/or identify common sounds and you can put extra provision in place.

Taking it forward

- For more excitement, you can make different ears, e.g. animal ears. This also encourages role play. Support listening by adding in additional tasks to the activity like 'Can all the rabbits hop when we hear a car?'.

- Allow the children to wear ears inside the setting to identify environmental noises, such as taps running.

What's that noise?

What you need:

- A selection of everyday objects that make sounds: whistle, squeaky toy, full pencil case, drum, rattle, etc.

What to do:

1. Sit a small group of children in a semicircle around the objects.

2. Demonstrate the sounds that each object makes when you hold it or move it in different ways.

3. Then, allow the children to play with objects and discover what sounds they make.

4. Next, ask the children to face away from you. Pick up each of the object in turn and move it so it makes a sound.

5. Nominate each child in turn to identify the sounds made.

What's in it for the children?

The children are learning to identify sounds and memorise auditory sequences.

Taking it forward

- You can extend the activity from a single sound by stringing different sounds together to make a short sequence, e.g. using a squeaky toy then a rattle.

- You can also allow the children to choose an object and make the sound for the others to guess.

Shake it all about!

What you need:

- Recycled containers: plastic tubs, bottles or small metal tins
- Materials for decorating: glitter, paint, paper, etc.
- Fastening agent: glue or sticky tape
- Small, dry materials: pasta, rice, sand, buttons, coins, etc.
- Low screen

What to do:

1. Allow children to choose a container to make into a shaker. They can decorate it too.

2. Offer children a range of material to fill their container with. Explain that different materials will make different sounds, e.g. sand might make a 'swooosh' sound and buttons might make a 'rattle' sound.

3. Children might want to make more than one shaker, filling each with a different material.

4. Allow children to play and experiment with their shakers. Encourage them to listen carefully to the different sounds they make.

5. Next, place the shakers behind a low screen. Shake each contain in turn and see if the children can identify whose shaker is producing the sound. What material do they think is inside it?

What's in it for the children?

The making of the shakers allows the children to actively experiment with how objects can produce sound and how this varies according to the different materials used.

Taking it forward

- Introduce a range of vocabulary as you make and play with the shakers by explaining the different materials you are using and what sounds they make.

- Model the language and then ask children to identify the sound using this language, e.g. 'It is a tin full of coins'.

Animal noises

What you need:

- Pictures or models of familiar animals that make distinct sounds such as a dog, cat, pig and cow

What's in it for the children?

This activity allows for the introduction of lots of basic vocabulary, e.g. animal names and habitats. It also supports sound discrimination and auditory memory.

Taking it forward

- You can gradually increase the number of animals and sounds you introduce in the circle.

- You can also hide the animals around the room. As children search for the animal, encourage them to remember and repeat the sound.

What to do:

1. Sit the children in a small circle.

2. Begin the activity by showing the children the toy or picture that represents each animal and modelling the sound it makes.

3. Next, put the animals in the middle of the circle and make the sound of one, e.g. 'Moo!'. Then choose one of the children to name or point to the animal.

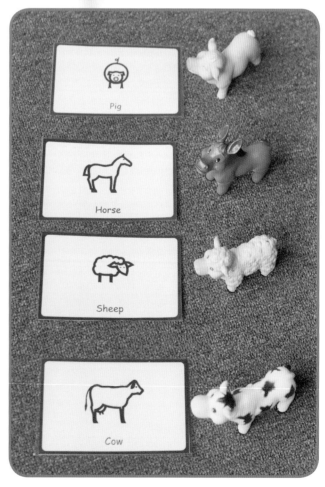

Circle sound game

What you need:

- An object that makes a clear and easily identifiable sound. This can be a homemade or a commercial object, e.g. a shaker or a squeaky toy

What to do:

1. Before the children are asked to play the game, ensure they have had time to listen to, and experiment with, the sounds you are going to use, for example as part of your role play area, at story time, etc.

2. Ask the children to make a circle.

3. Ask for a volunteer to sit in the centre and close their eyes.

4. The children then pass the object around the circle.

5. When the adult calls 'Stop!', the child holding the object clearly makes the sound.

6. Ask the child in the middle to point to where the sound is coming from.

7. These two children then swap places.

8. Ensure all children get a chance to sit in the middle of the circle.

What's in it for the children?

The children need to concentrate whilst in the main circle so that they can receive and pass on the instrument. This supports visual and auditory discrimination, as well as promoting cooperation and social development.

Taking it forward

- To challenge the children further, circulate more than one object around the circle at a time.

- The child in the middle can then try to identify sounds from two different directions.

Under the parachute

What you need:

- A large parachute
- A large, open space where children can run around safely

What to do:

1. Arrange the children around the parachute with adults interspersed to support.

2. Spend some time practising raising and lowering the parachute.

3. Ask the children to run underneath when the parachute is raised, if they can answer 'Yes' to the question asked. Ask questions about different criteria, e.g. 'Who has blue eyes?' and 'Whose favourite animal is a dog?'.

What's in it for the children?

This is a playful way to encourage listening skills. It can promote the understanding of positional language and the ability to follow instructions. It also encourages social interaction and cooperation.

The development of children's fine and gross motor skills are also supported by this activity, for example holding the parachute and finding different ways to move.

Taking it forward

- Make the questions more complex e.g. 'Who has brown hair and is wearing a jumper?'.

- Ask the children to move under the parachute in different ways. For example, you could give the instruction 'Jump under the parachute'.

- After modelling for several turns allow the children to give the instructions.

Who am I?

What you need:

- A blindfold, e.g. a sleep mask or scarf

What to do:

1. Get the children to form a circle. Go round the circle and ask each child to clearly say their name.

2. Ask a volunteer to stand, blindfolded, in the middle of the circle.

3. The children in the circle must walk around them.

4. When the adult calls out 'Stop!', the child in the middle must reach out and lightly touch the nearest child. The child must ask the blindfolded child, 'Who am I?'.

5. The child in the middle then tries to guess whose voice they have heard.

What's in it for the children?

This game promotes listening skills as the children are waiting for the 'Stop!' request. It also promotes social skills and expressive language, as the children communicate with each other through questioning and response.

Taking it forward

- Increase the number of children in the circle so the possibilities are increased.

When the music stops!

What you need:

- A CD player or MP3 player with easy to use Stop and Play controls
- A bank of familiar songs and tunes

What to do:

1. As part of your continuous provision, play the songs and tunes as part of the setting routine, e.g. at tidy up time, so the children are familiar with them.

2. Ask the children to form a circle.

3. Explain that they need to listen carefully and when the music stops they need to carry out the action you call out, such as clapping, jumping on the spot, sitting on the floor.

What's in it for the children?

This activity promotes listening skills because children need to respond to the stopping of the music. It also promotes cognitive development as children need to remember the action required when the music stops.

Taking it forward

- The children can take it in turns to stop and start the music.

- For further challenge, you can ask the children to perform two actions in a sequence, e.g. 'Sit down and clap three times'.

Threading beads

What you need:

- Long strings, laces or pipe cleaners
- A collection of easy to thread coloured beads

What to do:

1. Gather children in a small group.

2. Hand each child a pipe cleaner or thread.

3. Place the beads somewhere where they are easily accessed by all the children in the group, e.g. in the middle of the circle.

4. Call out instructions like 'Thread one red bead' and 'Now thread two blue beads'. Children have to follow your instructions to make a bead chain. Make one yourself simultaneously so you have a record.

What's in it for the children?

This activity encourages careful listening. It allows you to assess listening skills and understanding of both number and colour. Additionally, it supports the development of fine motor skills.

Taking it forward

- The instructions can gradually become more complex, e.g. 'Thread two green beads followed by two blue ones'.

Fruit salad

What you need:

- A range of plastic fruit, enough for every child to have a piece (ensure you have multiple of each fruit, e.g. two apples, two bananas)
- Chairs, enough for all but one child to have a seat

What to do:

1. Give each child a piece of fruit.
2. Ask the children to sit in a circle on their chairs facing inwards and to be ready to listen out to you calling out the names of different fruits.
3. One child must stand in the middle of circle.
4. Tell the children to listen for the name of their fruit to be called out, e.g. 'Oranges'. When they hear the name of their fruit they must get up and swap seats with someone else who has the same fruit.
5. If the child in the middle's fruit is called, they have to try and sit in one of the seats. This will leave a different child standing in the middle of the circle for the next round.

What's in it for the children?

This is a fun activity that helps children listen out for instructions and then follow them. It also promotes social and physical skills as children learn to cooperate and move safely in a small group.

Taking it forward

- Once you are confident that the children know the names of the fruit and have a good understanding of the game, you can add in a new instruction. Explain that when you call 'Fruit Salad' everyone must get up and find a new seat.

Household sounds

What you need:

- Models or pictures of a variety of household objects: hoover, tap, toilet, doorbell, phone, washing machine, toaster, etc.

- A recording of the sounds made by the objects above on a CD

What to do:

1. Spend some time with the children discussing the objects. As you talk, introduce lots of associated vocabulary such as 'dripping', 'ringing' and 'opening and closing'. Relate this talk to children's own experiences at home.

2. Next, play the tape and ask children to point to or name the object associated with that sound.

What's in it for the children?

This activity builds on the knowledge of household sounds, which the children should already have. It also encourages careful listening and supports children's oral communication.

Taking it forward

- Encourage the children to collect some classroom objects, for example a toy car. Help them to record the sound they make. Ask other children in the group to identify these sounds.

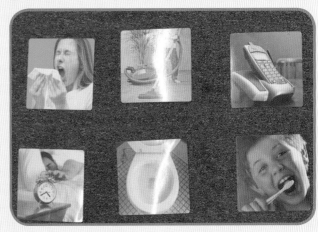

Choose a song

What you need:

- A selection of objects to represent favourite songs, such as a star for 'Twinkle, Twinkle Little Star', a toy bus for 'The Wheels on the Bus' and a spider for 'Incy Wincy Spider'

- Small chairs, one for each child

What to do:

1. For this activity, you will need the support of another adult.

2. Ask the children to sit on small chairs.

3. Offer the supporting adult a choice of two props. Ask them to choose one.

4. When the adult has chosen a prop, introduce the song that it corresponds to.

5. Sing the song together with the children and perform the actions as you sing.

6. Next, offer a child a choice of two props. When they have chosen, name the song that it corresponds to and sing it together.

What's in it for the children?

This activity helps children to start to understand that objects can be used to represent something else. This is an important stage in cognitive and language development. Encouraging the children to join in with the actions is another way of teaching them how to represent ideas.

Taking it forward

- You can start off by using real objects to represent the songs, then you can progress to using simple picture cards.

- Children may start to use an action or word to ask for their favourite song.

Posting!

What you need:

- A selection of photographs of real objects
- A post box (you can make this out of a recycled cardboard box)

What to do:

1. Show the child one picture at a time, name the picture and encourage the child to repeat the name.
2. Then, let the child post the picture into the box.
3. When you are confident that the child knows the names of the objects, show them two pictures.
4. Name one picture and see if the child can identify the correct picture and post it into the box.

What's in it for the children?

This activity will help children with their identification and naming skills. It is also a motivating way for children to learn simple vocabulary.

Taking it forward

- Use pictures of different categories, e.g. food, clothes, transport, animals. You can also use pictures of people carrying out different actions.
- Design the post box to a theme, e.g. it could look like an animal with a big mouth, so offer the child a choice of pretend food to 'feed' the animal.
- You can also use soft toys and puppets and ask the child to give the post box an object.

Fishing game

What you need:

- String
- A piece of dowel
- A small magnet
- A selection of pictures, laminated
- A handful of paper clips
- A pond or paddling pool, half filled with water

What to do:

1. Make a play fishing rod by tying string to a piece of dowel and attaching a small magnet to the end of the string. Ensure that the dowel is not sharp and that the magnet is firmly secured and is not a choking hazard.

2. Fasten a paper clip to each picture.

3. Float your selection of pictures in the pond or paddling pool.

4. Ask children to take turns using the fishing rod to fish a picture out of the pond. As they bring the picture out of the pond the adult supplies the name of the object pictured.

What's in it for the children?

This is a really good activity for developing children's vocabulary. Some children find it easier to store and remember the names of new or unfamiliar objects if they link them to the category, so adding a sorting element to the activity can support this.

Taking it forward

- You can use pictures from different categories. Then, as children fish pictures out of the pond, sort them into different categories, including clothes, toys and food.

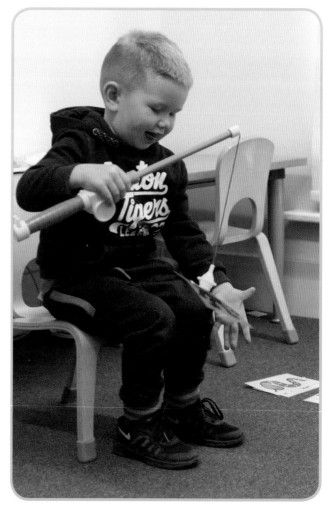

Tickle game!

- A feather duster - the 'tickle stick'

What to do:

1. Spend some time explaining what a feather duster is and what it is used for. This is a good opportunity to introduce some sensory language: 'soft', 'fluffy', 'feathery', etc.

2. Ask one child to be in charge of the tickle stick.

3. They need to choose another child, and also select a body part, to tickle.

4. As this is happening, label the body part they choose, e.g. 'Polly is tickling George's hand'.

5. Please ensure that you respect children's individual preferences in this activity, as some children will not want to be tickled in this way, whilst others will enjoy it immensely!

What's in it for the children?

This game teaches children the name of basic body parts. Children will learn how to listen to and follow simple instructions. Children can also learn to take turns in a small group. It is also great fun and will encourage laughter.

Taking it forward

- Instead of letting the child choose which body part to tickle, you can give the child a simple instruction. Tell them which body part to tickle and see if they follow the instruction.

- To make it more challenging, you could choose the child and the body part, so the child has to follow two elements in the instruction.

The spinner

What you need:

- Piece of card
- Arrow
- Split pin
- Velcro®
- Selection of 'action' pictures

What to do:

1. Make a large, but simple spinner using a circle of card, an arrow and a split pin.

2. Mark the spinner into sections and stick Velcro® onto each segment.

3. Stick pictures of different actions onto the spinner, e.g. going to sleep, brushing hair, washing hands, licking a lollipop or drinking from a cup.

4. Ask each child in turn to come and spin the spinner.

5. When the spinner stops, name the action using the word, and ask everybody to carry out the action. For example, if the image is going to sleep, then the children should all pretend to fall sleep.

Children learn simple action vocabulary by listening to and responding to adult modelling. It also promotes social development by encouraging children to wait and take their turn.

Taking it forward

- The spinner can be used to promote turn taking. To do this put a photo of each child on the spinner. The child whose photo the spinner stops on can take a turn.

- You can also use it to promote number correspondence. Write numbers on the spinner and whatever number it lands on, ask children to give you the corresponding number of grapes, marbles or other objects.

Story sounds

What you need:

- A story – you can use a book or make your own story up
- A selection of props that make a sound: a squeaky toy, a bell, coconut shells for horses' hooves, a rainmaker, a bag with a loud clasp, etc.

What to do:

1. Read the story with the children.
2. As you read, pause at certain moments when there is a sound, e.g. a door knocking or a dog barking.
3. Encourage the children to create the sound using the props.
4. You can also include the names of the children in the story to promote engagement.

What's in it for the children?

Telling and reading stories orally models story language, e.g. 'In the beginning…' and story structure (beginning, middle, end). This is an excellent foundation for children's later literacy development.

Taking it forward

- Gradually increase the length of the story and the number of sounds included. Decreasing the time between actions will further promote listening skills.

Slithery snakes!

What you need:

- Playdough
- Mats for children to model the playdough on
- Materials to decorate: glitter, beads, plastic eyes, etc.

What to do:

1. Allow the children to play with the playdough, exploring it with their hands. As they play, ask them how it feels.

2. Once they are familiar with the playdough, ask them to create a set of snakes of different lengths. Show them how to roll the playdough into the correct shape.

3. Ask the children if they can identify the longest and the shortest snake. Offer them a choice of two snakes to choose between.

4. For an extra challenge, ask them if they can place the snakes in size order.

5. Offer them decorating materials so they can make their snakes individual.

What's in it for the children?

This activity supports children's development of early mathematical concepts. It is also an excellent introduction to comparative language, e.g. 'long', 'longer' and 'longest'.

Taking it forward

- The same activity can be used introduce other comparisons, such as thin, thinner, thinnest and short, shorter and shortest.

Thumbs up/thumbs down!

What you need:

- A range of simple questions that the children can agree or disagree with, e.g. 'Am I wearing a blue jumper?'

What to do:

1. Show the children how to make a thumbs up response for 'Yes' and a thumbs down response for 'No'. Explain that these indicate agreement or disagreement.

2. In a small group ask some simple questions, such as 'Am I wearing a red jumper?', 'Is it dark outside?' and 'Do we come to school in our pyjamas?'. Tell the children that they have to respond visually by putting their thumbs up or down.

3. Once the children get used to the activity, it is a good idea to let them think about and ask the questions.

What's in it for the children?

This activity promotes careful listening skills and cognitive understanding. It might also be a useful way of assessing the listening and understanding skills of those children who are reluctant to speak.

Taking it forward

- This activity can be extended to reinforce prepositional language. For example, 'Am I standing in front of the door?'.

Themed guessing game

What you need:

- A story to introduce the theme
- A bag or box
- A set of objects that are connected to a theme, e.g. for 'The Seaside' you might have a bucket and spade, towel, swimsuit, goggles, rubber ring, etc. (It would be helpful to have these as part of your continuous provision)

What to do:

1. Introduce the theme to the children, e.g. by sharing a story.
2. Put the objects into a bag or box so that the children cannot see them.
3. Ask the children if they can identify each object by your description, for example 'I wear them to stop water splashing in my eyes'. When a child guesses correctly ask them to retrieve the object from the bag or box and show it the rest of the group.
4. Clearly articulate the name of each object as it is identified.

What's in it for the children?

This activity encourages the children to listen carefully and construct mental images from your descriptions. It also encourages children to make predictions which underpins later scientific understanding.

Taking it forward

- You can gradually make the clues more general, so the children need to wait for further clues such as 'It can go in the washing machine'.
- You can also make the language more difficult, e.g. 'You need to inflate this'.

Dressing up box

What you need:

- A selection of different coloured items of clothing: gloves, a scarf, jumper, coat, cardigan, slippers, etc.

What to do:

1. Ensure different clothing items are available to children as part of your continuous provision. For example, have a dressing up box in the role play area.

2. Play with the children as they explore items of clothing.

3. Then choose some of the clothes, and in a small group, ask a child to follow your instructions: 'Can you put on the green coat?', 'Can you find the red T-shirt?', 'Can you place the silver crown on your head?', etc.

4. You might also want to consider adding different sized clothing, for example baby clothes for dressing dolls and teddies. This will promote discussion about size: 'bigger', 'smaller', etc. You can also model tense usage, 'You are wearing a big jumper now but you wore a little jumper when you were a baby'.

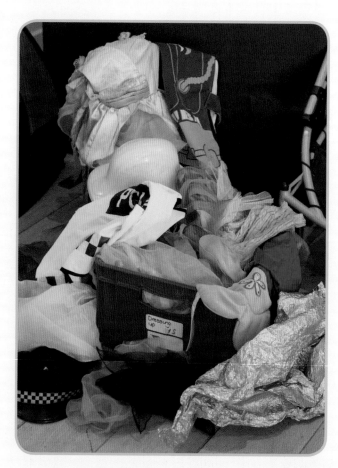

What's in it for the children?

This activity allows you to introduce some key everyday vocabulary such as the names for items of clothing and colours. It also supports children's ability to listen to and understand instructions.

Taking it forward

- For further challenge, you could ask the children to follow a sequence of two instructions, e.g. 'Can you put the red hat on your head, and find the yellow bag?'.

- After you have modelled a variety of instructions, you might ask children to give instructions to each other.

Going shopping

What you need:

- A section of items you might find in a shop: newspapers, magazines, empty sweet packets, plastic drink bottles, a bunch of plastic flowers, etc.
- A small plastic shopping basket

What's in it for the children?

This activity can introduce children to useful everyday language. You can assess children's listening and understanding skills in a fun interactive way.

Taking it forward

- Ask another child to role play as the shopkeeper.
- To help memory development, carry out the small group activity some distance from the shop. This means that the child must memorise the information for longer.
- You can adapt this idea to take place in the outdoor area, e.g. a garden centre.

What to do:

1. Before carrying out the group activity, set up a shop in the role play area. This will give children the experience of playing in the shop. Play with them and model different vocalarly. Additionally, if convenient, you might like to take the children to a suitable local shop – perhaps to buy something for the setting.

2. Choose a small group of children.

3. Place the objects in front of the children.

4. Spend some time talking to the children about the objects, and what they are, how they might be used and what kind of shop we might buy them from. This is a great opportunity to introduce lots of interesting vocabulary.

5. Then choose one child and ask them to buy a certain item and place it in the basket. You can ask for one or more items depending on the individual child.

6. Ensure all the children listen, have a turn and talk about the items.

Box game

- A robust cardboard box – it might be painted or decorated by the children and perhaps linked to your current theme, e.g. a treasure chest for a 'Pirates' topic or a kennel for an 'Animal' theme
- Some small toys or models related to your topic such as a big gold coin, a model of a pirate and a treasure map

1. With a small group of children, ask them to take turns to follow your instructions, for example 'Please put the gold coin inside the box', 'Please put the pirate next to the box' or 'Please put the gold coin underneath the box'.

What's in it for the children?

This is an active first-hand activity. It promotes understanding of prepositions with concrete objects. Linking action with concepts supports children's understanding.

Taking it forward

- You can ask the children to perform two consecutive actions, such as 'Please put the gold coin in the box and the pirate in front of the box'.

Bouncing balloons

What you need:

- A selection of inflated balloons

What to do:

1. In a small group allow the children some time to engage in free play with the balloons.

2. Whilst the children are enjoying this experience, consider how you might playfully interact with them and introduce descriptive language and words: 'light', 'floating', 'bouncing', 'inflate', etc. This will support children's spoken language development and later writing.

3. After a while, begin to direct their play by asking the children to gently move the balloons using a body part, e.g. 'Can you move the balloon using your hand/your knee/your elbow?'.

What's in it for the children?

This is activity promotes children's understanding and listening skills and introduces some key vocabulary, e.g. for body parts. The follow up activity promotes social skills and team-work.

Taking it forward

- Ask the children to work in pairs to carefully move the balloon about: 'Can you move the balloon together using your foreheads/ your hands/your tummies?'.

Getting the main idea

What you need:

- Mats with pictorial representation of different themes: a picture of a supermarket for food items, a picture of a school for classroom objects, a picture of a house for objects found in the home, etc.

- Pictures, models or objects of things from different categories: a can of soup (food), a pencil pot (classroom), a small saucepan (home)

- Counters

- Pots

What's in it for the children?

This activity encourages the children to listen carefully. It also helps them to develop the skill of categorisation, which supports later mathematical and scientific thinking.

Taking it forward

- To promote further discussion, choose an object that can be placed in more than one category, e.g. a book. In this example all the children can put a counter in their pot!

What to do:

1. Divide the children into small groups of two or three and give each group a different picture mat. You may want to start with two groups of children.

2. Spend some time talking about the picture mat so that the children understand the idea that the pictures represent a common category or theme, e.g. a school, a shop. Encourage them to talk about their relevant experience, if appropriate.

3. Ask the children, either individually or in a group, if they can name the different pictures on the mat in a particular category, e.g. the pencil pot on the school mat. This can be a very useful assessment opportunity.

4. Then show the children a new but related picture or object.

5. They need to identify if it falls into their theme or category. If they are correct, they put a counter in their pot.

6. Once they have collected a set number of counters (dependent on the age and ability of the children), the game is over.

Mime time!

What you need:

- A collection of pictures showing everyday actions: brushing hair, eating an apple, blowing up a balloon, putting on gloves, etc. Ensure the pictures contain a range of facial expressions such as looking happy, unhappy, facing difficulty

What to do:

1. Gather the children in a small group.

2. Ask one child to choose a picture, study it for a minute and then copy the action seen on the card in front of the other children, without speaking.

3. Ask the other children to guess what action the child is miming.

This activity helps children to understand that meaning can be communicated through both actions and words.

Taking it forward

- As the children become more experienced they might be able to suggest some actions themselves.

- You could also introduce relevant vocabulary and link to social development where appropriate: 'Why do you think they look happy/sad/tired in this picture?'.

Pairs

What you need:

- Some pictures or models that make pairs: dog and bone, spider and web, mouse and cheese, fishing rod and fish, knife and fork, needle and thread, cup and saucer, etc.

What to do:

1. Give the children a selection of photos showing objects/animals (or models) that are one part of a pair.

2. Talk to the children about the objects or animals, explaining clearly what each object/animal is and discussing its characteristics. Ask them to contribute by talking about their own experiences with the objects/animals.

3. Next, show them one of the corresponding objects/animals.

4. If the child correctly identifies it as part of their pair, they get to keep the object to make up a pair.

What's in it for the children?

This activity helps the children to listen carefully and begin to make links between objects/animals. It can also introduce useful vocabulary to support speaking and conversation skills.

Taking it forward

- To challenge the children further, gradually remove the pictures/models so that that activity becomes purely a listening activity. Read out the name of an object/animal, such as 'dog', and then give children a choice of two or three words, e.g. 'egg', 'bone', 'fish', to choose from. See if they can identify the word which makes a pair with the original word.

You choose

What you need:

- A parachute

What to do:

1. Introduce children to the parachute. Show them how to hold it and move it up and down as a group.

2. Model how to carry out certain instructions, e.g. 'Let's shake the parachute'.

3. If appropriate, you can then offer a supporting practitioner a choice, 'Shall we make it go up or down?', moving your hands up, then down. The supporting adult models making a choice using the word and moving his/her hands on the parachute and everybody joins in.

4. Then ask a child, 'Shall we shake or pull?', again using the parachute to show what the actions mean. The child can then use the action or the word to make their choice.

What's in it for the children?

Many children find it helpful when adults label an action before they have to make a choice. This enables them to carry out the action they have chosen, which will help them to remember the word linked to it.

Taking it forward

- Some children will need to play the game lots of times before the vocabulary and actions become familiar and they can join in. Repeat this activity regularly so they become comfortable with the actions and instructions.

Snack time

What you need:

- Laminated pictures of the different food choices available at snack time
- A laminated piece of cardboard
- Velcro®

What to do:

1. Stick the pictures of the food choices you have at snack time onto the laminated board using the Velcro®. Initially keep it simple – perhaps only offering a choice of two pictures.

2. Before snack time, show the children what food is available by taking them to the board. This will support them to make choices about what to eat.

3. Encourage them to point to the picture of the food or drink that they want.

4. Name the item that they point to and ask them to repeat the name back to you.

What's in it for the children?

This activity supports children's early communication and awareness of body language because it requires them to make gestures to make their wishes clear.

Taking it forward

- You can use these boards to offer choices at other times of the day too, e.g. play activities or song time.

Say what you see!

- A period of time when you can focus on the child's play, without interruption

What to do:

1. Look out for opportunities where children are engaged in self-initiated play and where you can introduce new vocabulary, consolidate existing language and extend grammatical understanding.

2. Start to model simple language linked to the actions the child is doing, e.g. 'Filling the jug, pouring the water, filling the jug…' or 'Splash! Splash! Ready steady... splash!'.

3. Pause and leave space for the child to copy any of the language you have modelled or to make a comment in return.

What's in it for the children?

This activity provides children with a structure in which language is clearly modelled. They can choose whether to join in or complete the phrases. This repetition is very helpful for young children as is the playful relaxed nature of the activity.

Taking it forward

- If the child responds to you and tries to engage in conversation, ensure you extend what they have said, e.g. the child might say 'Fish' and you could say 'Yes, a big fish' or 'The fish is swimming'.

Cosy spaces

What you need:

- A pop-up tent or a structure that can be covered with a sheet to create an enclosed space
- A small number of unusual or exciting resources that promote oral language: toys, books, games, props
- An imagination!

What to do:

1. Set up the tent in the quiet area. Fill it with exciting toys, books and games.

2. You could decorate the tent to reflect themes, e.g. for an 'In the Jungle' theme you might camouflage the tent and put in binoculars, a backpack, magnifying glasses and toy animals such as a monkey or a lion.

3. Let the children interact with the resources in the tent and help them use expressive language to describe their play.

What's in it for the children?

Calm and enclosed spaces provide privacy, which helps some children to use their expressive language. It also means that children are less distracted and can focus on their independent and imaginative play.

Taking it forward

- You could use a recording device so that children can share their adventures with the rest of the class. Recordings could also be played to parents.

Bag it!

What you need:

- A collection of different bags linked to activities: a carrier bag for shopping, a backpack for school, a sports bag for sports day
- A collection of objects associated with each bag: racket, ball, swimsuit or goggles

What to do:

1. Talk to the children about the different sorts of bags we might use for different purposes.

2. Pass a bag around the group and get the children to talk about its properties including size, colour, material.

3. Repeat this process with each bag.

4. Next, share the bags out among the children.

5. Introduce the collection of objects by naming each one clearly.

6. Then, ask the children to match each object with the correct bag. If they get the answer correct, they can add the object to their bag.

What's in it for the children?

This is a motivational way to support vocabulary acquisition and scaffold sentence formation. It also encourages expressive language.

Taking it forward

- Ask the children to repeat the name of the object and associated bag when they identify it, such as 'It's a swimsuit and it goes in my sports bag'.

Action words

What you need:

- A selection of everyday objects that have clear actions associated with them: a shoe to be tied, a toy car to be driven, a book to be read, a phone to be answered, etc.

What to do:

1. Put the objects in the middle of a circle of a small group of children.

2. Spend some time talking to the children about the objects. What are they? Who uses them? Where would we find them?

3. Next, mime the action that relates to each object, e.g. tying a shoelace.

4. Choose one child or ask the group to identify the object linked to your action. You can then ask the children to articulate a sentence in response to what they are seeing, e.g. 'What am I doing?', 'You are tying your laces' or 'You are brushing your teeth'.

What's in it for the children?

This activity helps to develop children's early understanding of how words work (grammar), such as 'doing' words. The linking of the action and the word promotes deep understanding.

Taking it forward

- You can get the children to model actions with other familiar objects in an everyday context.

- In time children can progress to suggesting their own objects and actions.

Role play

What you need:

- A large area of a setting, big enough for several children to play collaboratively together
- A collection of resources to reflect various themes, such as clothing or props
- An imagination!

What to do:

1. If possible, design your role play area around children's first-hand experiences including stories they have read, or trips they have made.

2. Role play areas can either be imitative, meaning that they are based on children's real-life experiences, e.g. a shop or a room in the home. Alternatively they can be imaginative to encourage a creative response, such as a spaceship, a castle or a pirate ship.

3. Role play provides an excellent context to sensitively introduce and model the use of relevant vocabulary.

4. Role play is also a really good way to acknowledge children's out of school interests, for example their hobbies and experiences of popular culture. So encourage the children to bring favourite items from home to use in this area, e.g. clothing and props from their favourite television characters.

What's in it for the children?

Dressing up and playing in role
supports the development of
children's expressive language.

Taking it forward

- Include the children in planning
  and resourcing the area. This will
  enable them to explore their own
  interests and draw on their own
  experiences.

Feely bag

What you need:

- A selection of objects that have interesting and diverse textures: rough (pine cone), smooth (plastic ball), soft (cuddly toy), furry (teddy), ridged (comb), metallic (key), etc.
- A bag or box

What to do:

1. Put the objects in the bag or box.
2. In a small group ask one child to choose an object and then give clues without naming the object. For the ball a child might say 'It's round', 'You can throw it', 'It can bounce on the ground', and so on.
3. Ask the other children try to guess which object they are describing after each individual clue.

What's in it for the children?

This is a playful activity that supports the development of children's descriptive language. This oral rehearsal supports writing development.

Taking it forward

- Challenge the children to source the objects in the bag themselves.
- Link this activity to a topic area, e.g. a fish, snorkel, flipper for the topic of 'Under the Sea'. This will support vocabulary development in this area.

Friends

What you need:

- A selection of homemade or bought heart shaped stickers

What to do:

1. Start the activity by talking about the kinds of positive things friends do for one another or by sharing an appropriate story.

2. Ask the children to give a sticker to someone who is a good friend to them. They have to explain why they think they are a good friend as they do this, i.e. they are kind, helpful, funny.

3. Repeat this activity so that you ensure that all the children in the group get a sticker.

What's in it for the children?

This activity gives the children a clear purpose for speaking. It also supports young children's social skills in terms of making relationships.

Taking it forward

- Allow the children to make their own stickers using labels. Encourage them to think of a range of positive reasons to give a sticker to someone. Let the children decorate their stickers.

Once upon a time

What you need:

- A range of books that tell traditional tales or nursery rhymes
- A selection of character masks related to the stories

What to do:

1. Choose a traditional tale to read to the children.

2. Encourage them to discuss what might happen next in the story. Support this by asking questions that check the children's listening and understanding.

3. Allow the children to role play the characters as you read the story. Provide them with masks to help them get into role.

What's in it for the children?

An understanding of characterisation and story sequence will prepare children for more complex skills, including reading and writing.

Taking it forward

- Leave the masks in the role play area to allow children the opportunity for free play. You can support this by encouraging them to sequence elements of the story in their play.

Detectives

- A selection of objects that can be easily linked to a person or animal: a cyclist (helmet, bicycle pump, tyre repair kit) or a dog (bowl, collar and lead and a rubber bone)

What to do:

1. Explain to the children that they are going to be detectives. Explain that some items have been found and we need to find out who they belong to.

2. Show them the objects, one at a time. Ask the children to name the objects as you show them.

3. Ask them if they can guess who has left these particular objects behind.

What's in it for the children?

This activity encourages children to problem solve. It also provides a stimulating purpose for talking.

Taking it forward

- The children might use Talking Tins or similar recording devices to make an oral list of the objects. They can then go around the classroom and see if other children can guess who they might belong to.

When I was a baby

What you need:

- A selection of baby photographs from all the children
- A story featuring a baby – you can use a book or make your own story up

What to do:

1. Ask parents and carers to talk about the photograph at home with the child before bringing it into the setting.

2. Start the activity by sharing an appropriate story that features a baby.

3. In a small group let the children share their photographs with one another.

4. One at a time ask a child to talk about what they are doing and wearing in their photograph. Help children to articulate how they have changed since the picture was taken.

What's in it for the children?

Children will feel a sense of ownership over the photograph and will have a breadth of knowledge about the content and context of it. This means that they will have lots of information to draw on when they talk about their photographs.

Taking it forward

- Parents and carers can enhance this activity by offering further details about the photograph. If possible, invite them to join in and schedule the activity to take place at a convenient time when they will be at the setting, e.g. just before children are collected at the end of the day.

The parcel

What you need:

- A variety of different shaped parcels (they should be easy to identify from their shape, e.g. frying pan, football, tennis racket, cup, plastic bottle)

What to do:

1. Talk to the children about their previous experiences of receiving and opening parcels.

2. Ask a small group of children to sit in a circle. Put the parcels in the middle.

3. Ask a child to choose one parcel. Let them investigate and talk about it. Scaffold the discussion with your questioning – 'Is it light?', 'Is it soft?' – and encourage the other children to ask questions too.

4. Let the child guess what it is and then open the parcel.

5. Then choose the next child to have a turn.

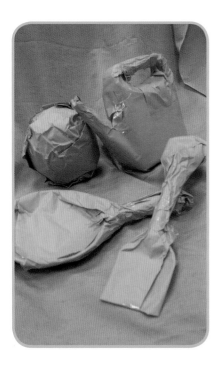

What's in it for the children?

This activity encourages children to think creatively, make predictions and draw on their existing knowledge. It also motivates them to ask questions.

Taking it forward

- You can extend this activity by making the contents of the parcels harder to guess, e.g. by putting them in rigid boxes tied with ribbon. However, ensure the shape, weight or feel of the parcel still provides a clue about what is inside.

50 fantastic ideas for early language development

Holiday packing

What you need:

- A suitcase
- A selection of clothing and accessories appropriate for hot, cold and wet destinations: flip flops, swimsuit, empty sun cream bottle, woolly hat, gloves, thick socks, scarf, rain coat, rain hat, umbrella, etc.
- An assortment of holiday objects: beach ball, bucket and spade, maps, etc.
- Postcards picturing a variety of holiday destinations

What to do:

1. Give the children the suitcase and a selection of clothes and holiday objects.
2. Then give them a postcard that shows somewhere hot, cold or rainy. Ask them to pack the suitcase in preparation for this holiday.
3. Model questions such as 'What do we need for somewhere rainy?' and 'What do we need for a day at the beach?'.

What's in it for the children?

This sorting activity encourages children to verbally categorise, make links and justify choices. It also introduces lots of interesting vocabulary.

Taking it forward

- Ask the children to pack for additional family members, e.g. an adult or a baby.

My favourite things

What you need:

- Empty shoeboxes
- A letter for parents and carers asking them to help with the activity at home

What to do:

1. Tell the children that you want to find out a little bit more about their favourite things.

2. Send each child home with an empty shoebox.

3. Include a letter to parents and carers asking them to help their child to fill the shoebox with a few of their favourite things (nothing too precious!).

4. Encourage parents and carers to have a discussion about why these things are meaningful to the child.

5. Ask parents and carers to bring the shoeboxes in to the setting the following day.

6. In small groups, get children to show the objects they have chosen and share why these objects are important to them.

What's in it for the children?

The children have chosen the objects themselves, so they should feel knowledgeable and confident telling others why they are important to them.

Taking it forward

- Let the children sit in pairs together and share the artefacts in their boxes. Encourage the children to ask each other questions.

Classroom instructions

What you need:

- A selection of audio recording devices: Talking Tiles, voice recorders

What to do:

1. Explain to the children that you want them to help you produce some recordings that provide information explaining how things are organised and how things work in the setting.

2. Give an example to demonstrate what kind of information you need, e.g. 'What would someone need to know about going outside to play?'.

3. Ask the children to talk about what someone would need to know. Can they create a list of instructions? Scribe this list for the children.

4. Finally help them to make a recording of these instructions. More confident children might want to read from the list for their recording.

What's in it for the children?

This activity gives children both a purpose and an audience for their talk. It also illustrates how the written word carries the oral meaning.

Taking it forward

- Use the written version of the oral instructions and explanations to create signs and labels to accompany the recording.

Puppet prompts

What you need:

- A story or poem
- Puppets (these can be homemade or bought)

What to do:

1. Ensure that the children are able to listen to a wide range of literature including traditional fairy tales, contemporary stories in which they see their lives reflected, and rhymes and poetry.

2. When you read to the children, ensure you explore the language of the characters, the vocabulary, intonation, pitch, etc.

3. Also spend some time helping the children to understand characterisation, for example why someone feels the way they do, or acts in a certain way.

4. Where appropriate, try to model story language like 'In the beginning', and make the children aware that stories have a structure: a beginning, middle and ending.

5. After hearing the story let the children play with the puppets, replicating and extending the story they have just heard.

What's in it for the children?

This is an ideal activity to promote and extend children's expressive dialogue.

Taking it forward

- Let the children choose their own story and make puppets for the different characters.